Vitamins

George Ivanoff

Smart Apple Media
P.O. Box 3263
Mankato, MN, 56002

First published in 2011 by
MACMILLAN EDUCATION AUSTRALIA PTY LTD
15–19 Claremont St, South Yarra, Australia 3141

Visit our web site at www.macmillan.com.au or go directly to www.macmillanlibrary.com.au

Associated companies and representatives throughout the world.

Copyright Text © George Ivanoff 2011

Library of Congress Cataloging-in-Publication Data has been applied for.

Publisher: Carmel Heron
Commissioning Editor: Niki Horin
Managing Editor: Vanessa Lanaway
Editor: Emma Short
Proofreader: Georgina Garner
Designer: Kerri Wilson
Page layout: Cath Pirret Design
Photo researcher: Sarah Johnson (management: Debbie Gallagher)
Illustrator: Leigh Hedstrom, Flee Illustration
Production Controller: Vanessa Johnson

Manufactured in China by Macmillan Production (Asia) Ltd.
Kwun Tong, Kowloon, Hong Kong
Supplier Code: CP December 2010

Acknowledgments
The author and the publisher are grateful to the following for permission to reproduce copyright material:

Front cover photograph: Boy eating grapes, Shutterstock/paulaphoto

Photographs courtesy of: Dreamstime, **8** (right), **18** (orange), /Alens, **10**, /Blinka, **26** (broccoli), /Broker, **14** (sardines), **27** (sardines), /Cybernesco, **3**, **7** (middle), **11**, /Denkyw, **14** (orange), /Draconus, **18** (almonds), /Elenathewise, **13**, /Fotoplanner, **26** (red peppers), /Fredredhat, **26** (cabbage), /Gudrun107, **26** (canteloupe), /Icefront, **7** (bottom left), /Irochka, **18** (broccoli), /Ivankmit, **18**, **26-7** (diary products), /Kennethman, **22**, /Lite, **18** (fish), **27** (fish), /Marylooo, **12**, /Monkey Business Images, **8**, /Rido, **18** (egg), /Riedochse, **27** (egg), /Tomboy2290, **26** (spinach), /Ukrphoto, **6** (bottom), /Valentyn75, **7** (bottom right), /Vlana, **26-7** (liver), /Wavebreakmediamicro, **23**; Getty Images/Tim Hall, **19**, /Jupiterimages, **15**; iStockphoto/Devan Muir, **26** (meat), /Nina Shannon, **29**; Photolibrary/ERproductions Ltd, **30**, /Ron Nickel, **4**, /Stockbrokerxtra Image, **9**; Pixmac/a4stockphotos, **6** (top), /Alexander Silaev, **7** (top); Shutterstock/Igor Dutina, **27** (nuts), /Elena Elisseeva, **26** (fruit), /Filip Fuxa, **28**, /Monkey Business Images, **5**, /Morgan Lane Photography, **6** (middle), /niderlander, **26** (seafood), /Martin Novak, **17**, /Patty Orly, **27** (soy milk), /Smileus, **26-7** (bread), /Gabriela Trojanowska, **24**.

Contents

When a word is printed in **bold**, you can look up its meaning in the Glossary on page 31.

What's in My Food?

Your food is made up of **nutrients**. Nutrients help your body work, grow, and stay alive.

Nutrients give you **energy** so you can be active.

Different types of food contain different types of nutrients. A **balanced diet** includes foods with the right amount of nutrients for your body.

A balanced diet helps keep your body healthy.

What Nutrients Are in My Food?

There are many different types of nutrients in your food. They include proteins, carbohydrates, fats, fiber, minerals, and vitamins.

Protein in meat, poultry, eggs and fish helps your body grow and heal.

Carbohydrates in bread and pasta give your body energy.

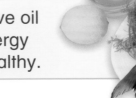

Fats in fish and olive oil give your body energy and help it stay healthy.

Fiber in bread and vegetables helps your body **digest** food.

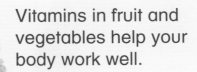

Vitamins in fruit and vegetables help your body work well.

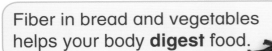

Minerals in milk and meat help your body grow and stay healthy.

Vitamins

Vitamins are nutrients that are found in many foods. They help your body grow, fight **infection**, and work well. Different people need different amounts of vitamins to stay healthy.

Age: 8

This person needs 0.0009 ounces (25 mg) of vitamin C each day.

Age: 60

This person needs 0.001 ounces (40 mg) of vitamin C each day.

Different types of food contain different types of vitamins. They also have different amounts of vitamins. Your body needs to get enough of each vitamin.

You need to eat foods that contain different vitamins every day.

What Are Vitamins?

Vitamins are found in foods made from plants and animals. There are two types of vitamins: fat-soluble vitamins and water-soluble vitamins.

Vitamin C is found in many foods, such as oranges.

Vitamins are **micronutrients**. Your body only needs small amounts of micronutrients to stay healthy.

Fruit and vegetables contain vitamins and minerals too, which are also micronutrients.

Fat-soluble Vitamins

Your body stores fat-soluble vitamins until they are needed. They are stored in your **liver** or in your **fatty tissue**.

Vitamins A, D, E, and K are fat-soluble vitamins.

Milk contains vitamins A and K.

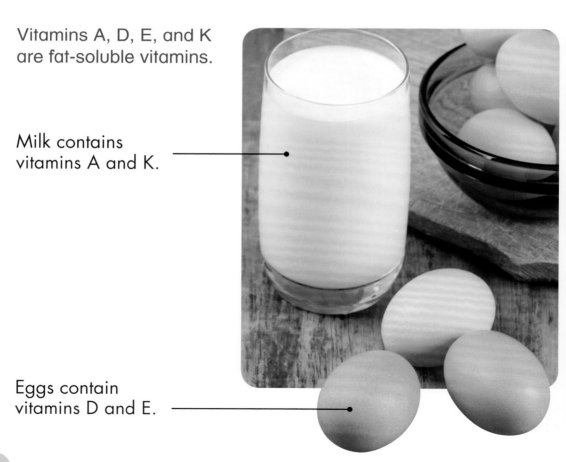

Eggs contain vitamins D and E.

Your body stores different fat-soluble vitamins for different amounts of time. Vitamin K is stored for a few days. Other vitamins can be stored for up to six months.

Green, leafy vegetables are a good source of vitamin K.

Water-soluble Vitamins

Your body uses water-soluble vitamins that it needs immediately. The rest pass out of your body in your **urine**.

Vitamins B and C are water-soluble vitamins.

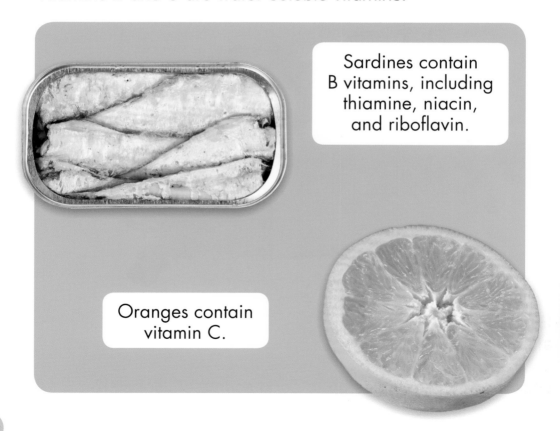

Sardines contain B vitamins, including thiamine, niacin, and riboflavin.

Oranges contain vitamin C.

You need to eat foods with water-soluble vitamins every day. Foods with these vitamins need to be stored carefully and cooked properly. Otherwise, their vitamins can be lost.

Strawberries should be stored in a refrigerator so they do not lose their vitamin C.

How Does My Body Get Vitamins?

Your body **absorbs** vitamins when you digest food. After food breaks down in your stomach, vitamins move through the wall of your intestine. The vitamins then enter your blood.

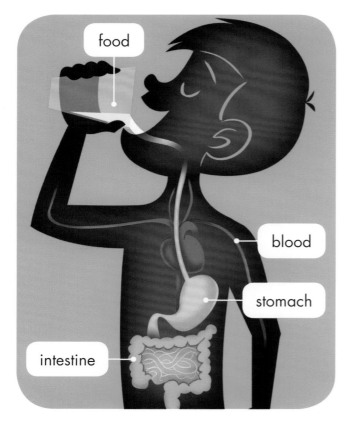

food

blood

stomach

intestine

Your blood carries vitamins all around your body.

Your body uses vitamins in different ways. It needs vitamins for growth and development but not for energy.

Your body gets energy from other nutrients, such as protein, carbohydrates, and fats.

What Do Vitamins Do?

Different vitamins do different things. Together they help your body grow, fight infection, and work well.

Different vitamins are found in different foods.

Vitamin

A

Vitamin

B

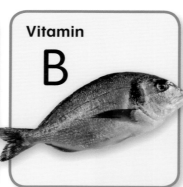

Vitamin

C

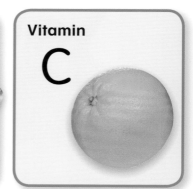

Vitamin

D

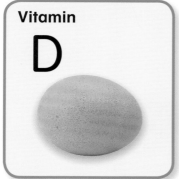

Vitamin

E

Vitamin

K

Vitamin A Helps My Eyesight

Vitamin A helps you see better. It also helps your body grow and your skin stay healthy.

Vitamin A helps you see at night and also helps you see colors.

Vitamin B Helps Me Get Oxygen

Vitamin B works with a mineral called iron to make red blood **cells**. Red blood cells carry **oxygen** around your body.

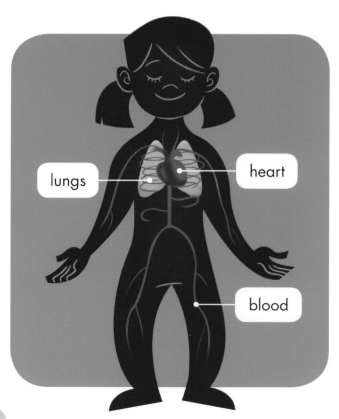

lungs

heart

blood

Vitamin B helps make red blood cells, which carry oxygen from your lungs around your body and back to your heart.

There are eight types of vitamin B. All the B vitamins are water-soluble.

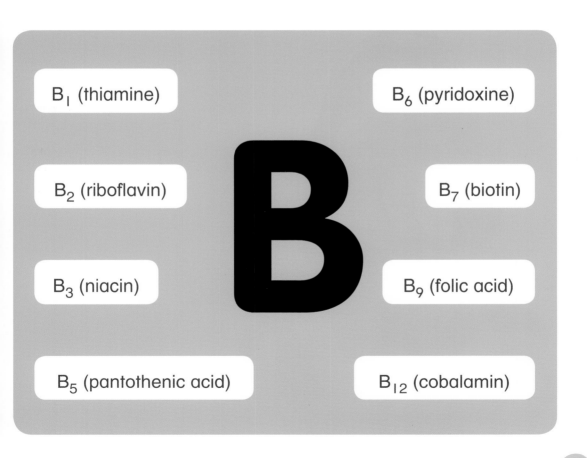

B_1 (thiamine)

B_6 (pyridoxine)

B_2 (riboflavin)

B_7 (biotin)

B_3 (niacin)

B_9 (folic acid)

B_5 (pantothenic acid)

B_{12} (cobalamin)

Vitamin C Helps Me Stay Healthy

Vitamin C helps your body fight infections, such as colds. It helps your body heal when it is hurt. It makes the walls of your **blood vessels** strong.

Vitamin C can't stop you from catching a cold, but it helps you get better.

Vitamin D Helps My Bones and Teeth

Vitamin D helps your body absorb a mineral called calcium. Calcium helps keep your bones and teeth strong.

Without vitamin D, your teeth and bones would be more likely to break.

Vitamin E Helps My Eyes, Skin, and Liver

Vitamin E helps keep your eyes, skin, and liver healthy. It also protects your body from illness, such as heart **disease**.

vitamin E cream

Your body can absorb vitamin E through your skin, as well as from eating food.

Vitamin K Helps My Blood Clot

Vitamin K helps your blood clot. When you cut yourself, you bleed. Your blood needs to clot to stop the bleeding.

When you cut your finger, blood cells stick together like glue to stop the bleeding.

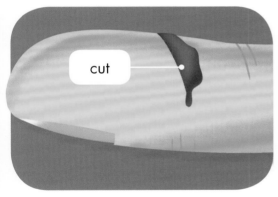

cut

1 Cut in finger starts to bleed.

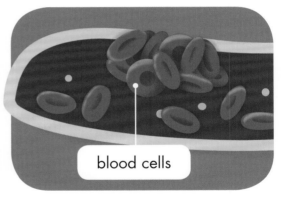

blood cells

2 Blood cells clot to stop the bleeding.

Which Foods Contain Vitamins?

Different foods made from plants and animals contain different vitamins. Your body uses them in different ways.

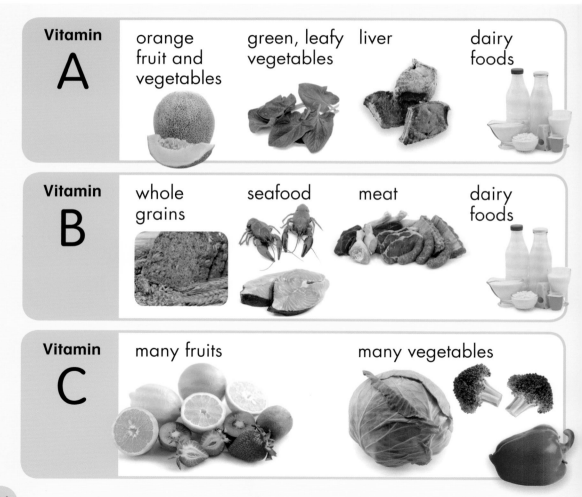

Vitamin A	orange fruit and vegetables	green, leafy vegetables	liver	dairy foods
Vitamin B	whole grains	seafood	meat	dairy foods
Vitamin C	many fruits		many vegetables	

You need to eat foods with vitamins every day.

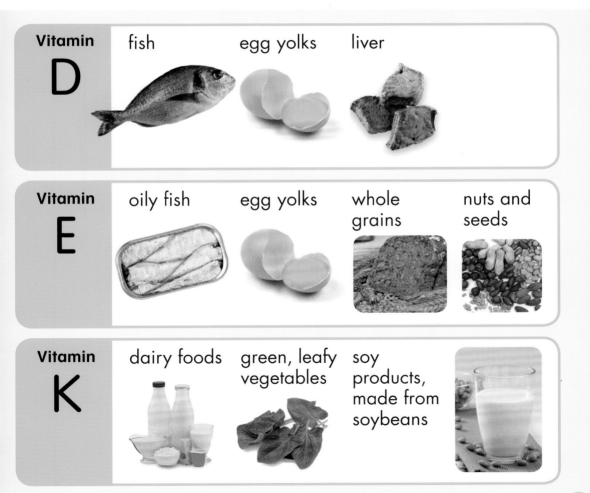

Vitamin D
fish   egg yolks   liver

Vitamin E
oily fish   egg yolks   whole grains   nuts and seeds

Vitamin K
dairy foods   green, leafy vegetables   soy products, made from soybeans

Vitamin Supplements

Some people take vitamin **supplements**, although most people do not need them. Supplements can help people who do not have a balanced diet.

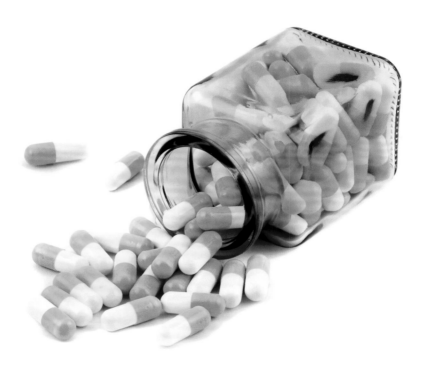

Many **vegans** take vitamin supplements, because they don't eat meat, poultry, fish, or dairy foods.

Taking too many vitamin supplements can be unhealthy. Having too many vitamins in your body can cause as many problems as not having enough.

It is always healthier to get vitamins from food, not supplements.

What Happens if I Don't Eat Vitamins?

If you don't eat vitamins, your body won't work well. Cuts and scrapes won't heal. You will get sick more often. You might get **tooth decay**.

Without vitamins, your bones would not be as strong and could break more easily.

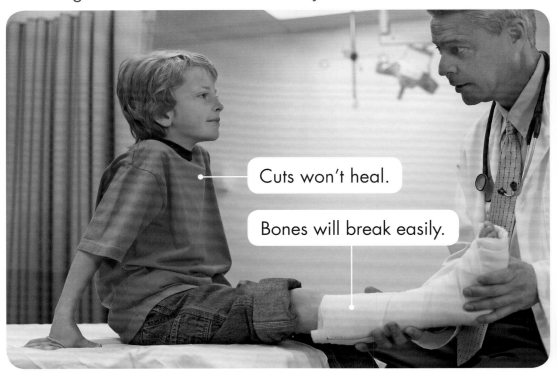

Cuts won't heal.

Bones will break easily.

Glossary

absorbs	takes in
balanced diet	a healthy selection of food that you eat
blood vessels	the tubes that your blood travels through
cells	the smallest living parts of a living thing
digest	to break down food in the body
disease	an illness or sickness
energy	the ability to be active
fatty tissue	parts of your body where fat is stored
infection	the spread of germs or a disease
liver	the part of your body that stores vitamins
micronutrients	nutrients that your body needs in small amounts
nutrients	the healthy parts of food that people need to live
oxygen	a gas in the air that living things need to breathe
supplements	vitamins taken as tablets, capsules, liquid, or powder
tooth decay	damage to your teeth caused by sugar and acid in food
urine	liquid material that passes out of your body
vegans	people who do not eat food made from animal products

Index